D1710844

DEF LEPPARD

Arena Rock Band

Library Ed. ISBN-13:
978-0-7660-3031-2
Paperback ISBN-13:
978-0-7660-3623-9

Library Ed. ISBN-13:
978-0-7660-3236-1
Paperback ISBN-13:
978-1-59845-210-5

Library Ed. ISBN-13:
978-0-7660-3379-5
Paperback ISBN-13:
978-1-59845-212-9

Library Ed. ISBN-13:
978-0-7660-3232-3
Paperback ISBN-13:
978-1-59845-211-2

Library Ed. ISBN-13:
978-0-7660-3234-7
Paperback ISBN-13:
978-1-59845-208-2

Library Ed. ISBN-13:
978-0-7660-3028-2
Paperback ISBN-13:
978-0-7660-3620-8

Library Ed. ISBN-13:
978-0-7660-3029-9
Paperback ISBN-13:
978-0-7660-3621-5

Library Ed. ISBN-13:
978-0-7660-3027-5
Paperback ISBN-13:
978-0-7660-3619-2

Library Ed. ISBN-13:
978-0-7660-3026-8
Paperback ISBN-13:
978-0-7660-3618-5

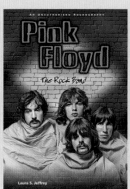

Library Ed. ISBN-13:
978-0-7660-3030-5
Paperback ISBN-13:
978-0-7660-3622-2

Library Ed. ISBN-13:
978-0-7660-3233-0
Paperback ISBN-13:
978-1-59845-213-6

Library Ed. ISBN-13:
978-0-7660-3231-6
Paperback ISBN-13:
978-1-59845-209-9

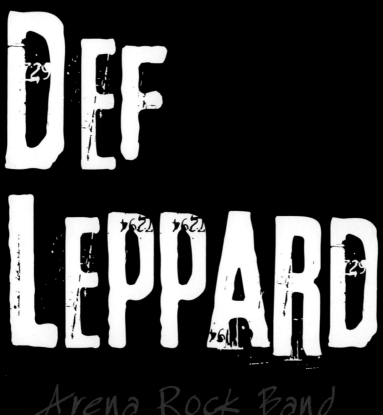

DEF LEPPARD

Arena Rock Band

Laura S. Jeffrey

REBELS OF **ROCK**

E **Enslow Publishers, Inc.**
40 Industrial Road
Box 398
Berkeley Heights, NJ 07922
USA

http://www.enslow.com

Library of Congress Cataloging-in-Publication Data

Jeffrey, Laura S.
    Def Leppard : Arena Rock Band / Laura S. Jeffrey.
        p. cm. — (Rebels of rock)
    Includes bibliographical references, discography, and index.
    Summary: "A biography of British rock band Def Leppard"—Provided by publisher.
    ISBN-13: 978-0-7660-3234-7
    ISBN-10: 0-7660-3234-5
    1. Def Leppard (Musical group)—Juvenile literature. 2. Rock musicians—England—
Biography—Juvenile literature. I. Title.
    ML3930.D37J44 2010
    782.42166092'2—dc22
    [B]   2008040363

ISBN-13: 978-1-59845-208-2 (paperback ed.)

Printed in the United States of America

052010 Lake Book Manufacturing, Inc., Melrose Park, IL

10 9 8 7 6 5 4 3 2 1

To Our Readers: This book has not been authorized by Def Leppard or its successors.

We have done our best to make sure all Internet Addresses in this book were active and appropriate when we went to press. However, the author and the publisher have no control over and assume no liability for the material available on those Internet sites or on other Web sites they may link to. Any comments or suggestions can be sent by e-mail to comments@enslow.com or to the address on the back cover.

Every effort has been made to locate all copyright holders of material used in this book. If any errors or omissions have occurred, corrections will be made in future editions of this book.

♻ Enslow Publishers, Inc., is committed to printing our books on recycled paper. The paper in every book contains 10% to 30% post-consumer waste (PCW). The cover board on the outside of each book contains 100% PCW. Our goal is to do our part to help young people and the environment too!

Photo Credits: © Johnathan Barton/iStockphoto, p. 10; BBC Photo Library/Redferns, p. 42; Brendan Beirn/Rex Features, p. 19; George Chin, pp. 22, 54; Andre Csillag/Rex Features, pp. 6, 21; Ian Dickson/Redferns, p. 50; GAB Archives/Redferns, p. 46; Patrick Harbron/Landov, p. 40; Hulton Archive/Getty Images, p. 15; Mick Hutson/Redferns, pp. 17, 60; © Mary Evans Picture Library/Roger Mayne/The Image Works, p. 26; PRNewsFoto/Live Nation, p. 80; PRNewsFoto/Universal Music Enterprises, p. 78; © VH1/Courtesy: Everett Collection, p. 63; WireImage/Getty Images, pp. 30-31; WpN/Photoshot, p. 73.

Cover Photo: Robert Knight. (Def Leppard in 2000.)

CONTENTS

Def Leppard in 1981. From left to right: Rick Savage, Steve Clark, Rick Allen, Pete Willis, Joe Elliott.

A FREAK ACCIDENT

The weather in Sheffield, England, was unseasonably mild on December 31, 1984. It was the perfect day for Rick Allen to take a drive in his expensive, new sports car. Allen was only twenty-one years old, but he had already experienced incredible success. He had started playing the drums when he was a child, and when he was only fifteen years old, he had dropped out of school to become drummer for the newly formed heavy-metal band Def Leppard.

Def Leppard would become famous for their rock anthems that combined powerful and loud electric guitars with catchy melodies and sing-along, let's-have-a-party lyrics. Already, the group had released three albums and toured around the world. The group's songs were playing on the radio, and their music videos were in heavy rotation on the fledgling Music Television channel (MTV). Allen and his bandmates, who were not much older than he was, had become close friends who were enjoying all the benefits that came with being a successful band.

But it had not all been so easy. The group was much more popular in the United States than in their native England because many British music fans believed Def Leppard had "sold out" to America and didn't look or sound "heavy metal" enough.[1] Then, during production on Def Leppard's third album, founding member and guitarist Pete Willis was fired because of his uncontrollable drinking.

The remaining band members hired Phil Collen to replace Willis and then turned their attention to a fourth album. They wanted to work with producer Mutt Lange because he had helped them achieve phenomenal success with their last two albums. But Lange was unavailable, so they hired another producer. From the start, the band and their new producer clashed over creative issues. After months of increasing tension, Def Leppard fired this producer and decided to produce the record on their own. They moved their operations from a recording studio in Ireland to a studio in Holland.

Finally, with the New Year approaching, the group was only a few months from completing the album. In fact, Allen had already finished recording most of the drum tracks. The band was taking a break for the holidays, and Allen was in his hometown visiting his parents.

On the morning of December 31, 1984, Allen decided to go for a ride with his then-girlfriend Miriam Barendsen. She was from Holland, and he wanted to show her the scenic Ladybower Reservoir. The couple removed the sunroof from Allen's Corvette Stingray, climbed into the car, fastened their seatbelts, and headed out of town on A57 Manchester Road.

On their way back into town, Allen and Barendsen encountered another sports car on the narrow, winding road. The car passed Allen, then slowed down, but then sped up when Allen tried to drive around it. After a few miles of following the sports car, Allen pushed hard on his accelerator so that he could pass. He continued to travel at a dangerously high speed. Suddenly, Allen came to a particularly sharp curve and lost control of the car. The car slammed into a brick wall and flipped over.

Barendsen was badly bruised, but her injuries were minor. The Def Leppard drummer was not as fortunate. Allen was thrown from his sports car. As he flew out, the seatbelt acted like a knife, severing his left arm just below the shoulder.[2] His right arm was also badly injured.

Two nurses, one who lived near the crash scene and another who happened to be driving by, rushed to the couple's aid. They helped Barendsen out of the car, and they bandaged Allen's shoulder where his left arm had once been so that the

ON DECEMBER 31, 1984, RICK ALLEN TOOK A DRIVE
WITH HIS GIRLFRIEND TO LADYBOWER RESERVOIR. IT WAS
HERE WHERE HIS CAR ACCIDENT TOOK PLACE.

drummer would not bleed to death. They also found Allen's
arm, wrapped it, and placed it in ice to keep the tissue alive.
The nurses knew it was possible to reattach severed limbs. An
ambulance quickly arrived on the scene and rushed Allen and
Barendsen to nearby Royal Hallamshire Hospital.

"I've seen the whole accident in my head," Allen said
later. "But it's difficult to explain. There really wasn't any
sensation. It was like my whole body was numb, tensed. There
was no pain, no nothing. Just emptiness."[3]

News of the accident spread quickly among Allen's bandmates. Guitarist Rick "Sav" Savage was at his home in

Sheffield when he received a phone call from band manager Peter Mensch. Savage's home was very close to the hospital. Allen's parents soon walked over from the emergency room to update Savage on Allen's condition.[4]

Lead singer Joe Elliott, another Sheffield native, was at his home in London when he received the grim news. Guitarists Steve Clark and Phil Collen were reached in Paris, where they both kept apartments. "I really wanted the whole lot of us to be in one room, just to be able to talk, I guess," Elliott recalled later. "We're always together, working, recording, touring, and you begin to take it for granted. This was one time I wanted us to be together, and it was impossible."[5]

Allen spent several hours in surgery. Doctors were able to repair the damage in his right arm, and they reattached Allen's left arm. For awhile, it looked as though the surgery had been a success. But a few days later, Allen's left arm became infected and had to be removed permanently. Savage remembers thinking, "How's he gonna live the rest of his life if he can't play drums? That's all Rick had ever done."[6]

"To me, this guy was the best rock drummer in the world," Elliott said. "And in that [hospital] bed, I was seeing a body that would never work the same again. I felt so bad for him, because I knew how much playing the drums meant to him."[7]

Allen himself was also feeling very depressed, despite visits from his bandmates and cards he received from fans around the world. Allen was worried that he would never be able to play the drums again.[8] For awhile, he did not think he would even live through the recovery. "At a certain point, I didn't think I was going to make it," he recalled later. "I felt like it wasn't time [to die]. I felt like I had so much to do."[9]

The other band members were relieved Allen had survived. "We're just glad he's alive," a band spokesman said.[10] However, they had many questions about the future of Def Leppard. Should the bandmates try to finish the fourth album without their drummer? What about a temporary replacement— or did they need to face reality and find a permanent replacement? After all, as Joe Elliott remembers thinking, "Who ever heard of a one-armed drummer?"[11] Or perhaps it was time for Def Leppard to break up. Would they, could they, go on without Allen?

The days, weeks, and months ahead would prove to be very challenging ones for the group. Though Allen's horrific accident was not the first challenge the band had faced in its years together, it was certainly the biggest. But as time would prove, it would not be the last.

THE DEF LEPPARD LINEUP

All the original members of Def Leppard hail from Sheffield in South Yorkshire, England, or the nearby suburbs. The working-class city is best known for its industrial roots; factories have produced steel for hundreds of years. But since the 1960s, Sheffield has also been known as the hometown for musicians who have found success on the worldwide stage.

The first Sheffield native to make it big in music was rock and blues singer Joe Cocker. Cocker is a gruff-voiced singer who started his career in the 1960s. Perhaps best known for covering Beatles songs, he performed during the 1969 Woodstock Festival in New York. (Cocker had a comeback in the 1980s and 1990s with several hits songs, including "Up Where We Belong," a duet with Jennifer Warnes that was featured in the movie *An Officer and a Gentleman*; "You Are So Beautiful"; "You Can Leave Your Hat On"; and "When the Night Comes.")

The members of Def Leppard came after Cocker, and their success paved the way for other bands with Sheffield roots, including the Thompson Twins, Arctic Monkeys, Little Man Tate, and the Aboriginals. Here is a look at the members of Def Leppard.

Richard John Cyril "Rick" Allen

Richard John Cyril "Rick" Allen is the youngest of the Def Leppard band members. He was born on November 1, 1963, in Derbyshire, a suburb of Sheffield, England. As a young child, he would wake up on Sunday mornings to hear the Salvation Army band marching down his street. "I'd put my clothes on, I'd run out and I'd literally march down the street with them next to the guy with the big drum," he said. "It just touched me in a really deep way . . . the feeling of the drums and what it did to me."[1]

When Rick was eleven, his parents bought him a drum set. Every morning, he woke up and played the drums before he did anything—even before he put on clothes. He recalled "falling out of bed in the morning as a kid, and being completely naked. . . . It wasn't that I enjoyed being naked, it's just

Rick Allen
in 1987

that I was lazy, and I didn't bother to put anything on."[2] Eventually, he became accustomed to playing the drums while wearing clothes. However, he still plays barefoot. "I [became] used to the feeling of just playing the drums that way and the fact that I felt so connected to the drums doing it that way," he said.[3] By the time he was twelve, Rick had formed a band with neighborhood friends and was playing in clubs for money. Always more interested in music than in school, Rick dropped out of high school at the age of fifteen to become the drummer for Def Leppard. His older brother Robert became Def Leppard's sound man and road manager—and Rick's chaperone.

Joseph Thomas "Joe" Elliott

Joseph Thomas "Joe" Elliott was born on August 1, 1959, in Sheffield. When he was five years old, he heard his first Beatles song. That was when he knew he wanted to be a rock-and-roll musician.[4] He learned to play drums and the guitar, and he daydreamed about being in a band.

"When I was in school in Sheffield, I used to write imaginary reviews of gigs that never happened, instead of writing English essays," he said. "In art, instead of a vase full of flowers, I'd draw posters with imaginary bands on them."[5] He added, "I figured out fairly early that I wasn't gonna be a brain surgeon or nuclear physicist. So I fantasized about rock & roll."[6]

Joe Elliott
in 1990

Elliott became Def Leppard's lead singer because the band already had two guitar players.

Richard "Sav" Savage

Guitarist Richard "Sav" Savage was born on December 2, 1960, in Sheffield. He was the youngest of three boys born to Kenneth, a newspaper typesetter, and Sally Savage. When he was about eleven years old, his brother John taught him how to play "Maggie May" on an old acoustic guitar. That song was written by British singer-songwriter Rod Stewart.

"I didn't know a D from an A," he said. "But the songsheet had these chord boxes that told you where to put your fingers. Within the evening, I'd learned the whole song. I was strumming away and singing miles out of key."[7]

Savage was also a gifted soccer player and considered playing the sport professionally. But after meeting Pete Willis, who was a grade ahead of him at Tapton Comprehensive School, music became more important. The two jammed and played in local clubs. After they each had graduated, they formed a band called Atomic Mass. Their band never landed any paying gigs, and they played mostly covers of songs by Irish hard-rock band Thin Lizzy and British rock bands Led Zeppelin and Bad Company. Atomic Mass formed the core of what became Def Leppard.

Savage plays bass guitar and contributes vocals for Def Leppard. He also plays guitar, keyboards, and the synthesizer.

Rick Savage
in 1992

He adopted the nickname "Sav" to distinguish him from the other "Rick" in Def Leppard, drummer Rick Allen.

Peter Andrew "Pete" Willis

Savage's classmate and Atomic Mass bandmate, Peter Andrew "Pete" Willis, was born on February 16, 1960, in Sheffield. At the age of eight, he made a play guitar after seeing American guitarist, singer, and songwriter Jimi Hendrix on television.[8] By the time Pete was twelve, his parents had bought him a real electric guitar, and he learned how to play it.

Willis was with Def Leppard for the group's first three albums. He cowrote many of the songs, played the guitar, and contributed vocals. However, he developed a drinking problem that got out of control, and it led to increasing tension with his bandmates. Willis was fired from the band.

"Pete was a really nice guy when he didn't drink, and he was a really good guitar player," Joe Elliott once said. "Pete probably still is a really good guitar player, and he probably still is a really nice guy when he's sober. The problem is that he was very rarely sober after 7 P.M."[9] Willis later said that he was somewhat relieved when he was asked to leave the band.[10]

Philip Kenneth "Phil" Collen

Guitarist Philip Kenneth "Phil" Collen was hired to replace Willis. He was born on December 8, 1957, in a working-class neighborhood of London. His father was a truck driver and his

Pete Willis
in 1981

Steve Clark and Phil Collen in 1983

mom was a housewife. As a child, Phil swam and played soccer, but music was his first love. When he was fourteen years old, his parents took him to a Deep Purple concert. "I remember going to see Purple playing live and seeing [guitarist Ritchie Blackmore] in action," he said. "I was just astonished and thought, 'I wanna do that.'"[11]

Two years later, he received an electric guitar for his sixteenth birthday and began taking lessons. He left school and held a variety of low-paying jobs while playing music on the side. He was in glitter-rock groups Dumb Blondes and Girl before joining Def Leppard.

Glitter rock, also known as glam rock, featured campy, theatrical aspects, with band members wearing lots of makeup. Girl was especially well-known on the British music scene, and it was big news when Collen left. After joining Def Leppard, Collen became one of the group's main songwriters.

Stephen Maynard "Steve" Clark

The final original member of Def Leppard is Stephen Maynard "Steve" Clark. He was born on April 23, 1960, in the Sheffield suburb of Hillsborough. He was the oldest son of Barry, a cab driver, and Beryl Clark. When he was eleven years old, Steve's father bought him his first guitar, and he began taking lessons. He learned Led Zeppelin and Thin Lizzy songs as well as classical pieces by Bach and Vivaldi.[12] He was taking college classes and playing guitar with a cover band called Electric

Chicken when he met Pete Willis, who invited him to audition for Def Leppard.

Clark made many valuable contributions to Def Leppard. He had several nicknames, including "Steamin' Steve," for his energetic style of performing, and "the Riffmaster," because of the brilliant guitar riffs and hooks he created for now-classic Def Leppard songs, including "Foolin'" and "Photograph." Riffs are rapid and often improvised series of notes, and hooks are devices to grab the attention of listeners.

"There would be times when Phil or Sav would come in with a complete song that was good, but Steve would say, 'Well, why don't we do this with it?'" Elliott said. "And he would turn a good song into a great song."[13]

However, like his bandmate Willis, Clark also battled with alcohol. In fact, he also had another nickname—he and guitarist Phil Collen were called "the terror twins" because of their hard-partying ways.

Clark would "be so quiet offstage," Elliott said. "Then he would get up there and explode into this guitar god. That was his thing. He didn't have any hobbies whatsoever. He did crosswords. That was the nearest thing he had to something outside of the band. But his guitar was it. Playing his guitar and having a drink afterward—those were the two most important things in his life."[14] Unfortunately, Clark's addiction had fateful consequences for himself as well as the band.

3

HELLO AMERICA, HELLO WORLD

The roots of Def Leppard began in 1977. Guitarist Pete Willis and bass guitarist Rick Savage had graduated from high school and were holding down low-paying jobs and playing music on the side. Their band, Atomic Mass, had no paying gigs, and Willis and Savage were unhappy with their lead singer. Additionally, they wanted to do more than just play covers of hits by other bands. They wanted to write their own songs.

One night, Willis ran into Joe Elliott in Sheffield. The two were acquaintances and began talking. Elliott had also graduated from high school and was driving a van for a living, but he wanted to be in a band.

MEMBERS OF DEF LEPPARD MET IN SHEFFIELD, ENGLAND, SEEN HERE IN 1961.

He even had a band name: Deaf Leopard. It was something Elliott had thought of as a boy, when he was fantasizing about being in a rock-and-roll band instead of completing his school assignments. Elliott had even kept the posters he had drawn of a leopard wearing an oversize earring.

Willis invited Elliott to meet with him and Savage and talk about starting a new group. Elliott "had the posters, he had the idea and he had the name," Savage recalled. "After a while, it started to sound pretty good to me."[1] Willis and Savage agreed to the new band name, but they decided to change the spelling. At the time, punk rock was big on the music scene, and several punk-rock groups had incorporated animals into their band names. Elliott, Willis, and Savage changed the spelling to Def Leppard so their band would not be confused as a punk-rock group.

Later, some people thought they changed the spelling so that it would sound like Led Zeppelin. Band members said that was not the intention, though they admitted they were influenced musically by the English heavy-metal band. Led Zeppelin songs, such as the now-classic "Stairway to Heaven," have been described as beginning with peaceful acoustic guitars that evolve into mean-minded power chords.[2]

The Def Leppard musicians scraped some money together and rented space in an old spoon factory in Sheffield. Rehearsals began in November 1977. Elliott became the lead singer because Willis and Savage were better on guitar than he was. Tony Kenning, who had been with Atomic Mass, played the drums. "It was pretty weird," Elliott recalls. "We'd play until four A.M., go home, get about an hour's sleep, then go to work. I used to hide under a mound of boxes and sleep at work."[3]

Things were coming together, but the band members thought they needed someone who was strong on guitar solos. A couple of months later, Willis and Elliott were at a Judas Priest concert in Sheffield when they ran into Steve Clark. Judas Priest was a very influential heavy-metal band from Birmingham, England.

Willis and Clark knew each other from a college class they were both enrolled in. "I used to see him reading a guitar book, so I thought he must play guitar," Willis said.[4] They told Clark about Def Leppard and invited him to audition for the band. Clark impressed them with his superior guitar skills, so now he, too, was in.

For the next several months, the musicians wrote songs and spent a lot of time—maybe even too much time—rehearsing. "I was itching to gig," Clark said. "We were rehearsing for three hours a night but the others seemed happy to keep doing that. One night . . . I said I'd had enough . . . and threatened to quit the band if we didn't play a gig soon."[5]

Elliott asked around and in July 1978, he landed the band a show at Westfield School in Sheffield. They played a few other gigs before deciding to make their own record. They borrowed money from Elliott's parents to pay for the time at the recording studio.

Shortly before Def Leppard was scheduled to record, Kenning left the band. "I think his girlfriend at the time had a lot to do with it," Savage said. "She didn't like him messing around with the band. He was always a quiet sort of person anyway. He never had anything to do with the writing. Maybe he felt left out. I don't think his heart was in it like the rest of us."[6]

The remaining Def Leppard members hired Frank Noon to play drums on the record, but Noon was never an official member of the band. The bandmates ran an ad for a new drummer, and fifteen-year-old Rick Allen answered it. Even though Rick was a few years younger than the others, he actually had more professional experience.

During his audition, "We asked Rick if he knew *Emerald* [a song] by Thin Lizzy," Savage recalled. "We played that and suddenly the song sounded six times better than the way we usually played it. We were now in the company of a proper drummer. Even at fifteen, he was outstanding."[7] Allen officially became a member of Def Leppard in November 1978.

The group's debut album, *The Def Leppard EP,* came out in January 1979. The album had three songs on it, and the band paid to have one thousand copies made. "Me and my mum glued" all the sleeves that held the records, Elliott recalled. "I photocopied the lyric sheets at work, during my dinner hour, illegally, folded them up, slipped them in the thing, and the first 100 went with lyric sheets."[8] Those early discs are now a rare and valuable collector's item.

Elliott took charge of Def Leppard marketing efforts. He gave the records to disc jockeys at local radio stations and critics at music magazines. He organized the selling of records after shows. Elliott also wrote letters to music critics for newspapers and magazines, inviting them to come hear the new band. One music critic recalled attending a gig at a Sheffield club. He said Def Leppard "came on stage and were mightily impressive. . . . We could see there was definitely something there."[9]

The band gained even more exposure when their record

was played on BBC radio. In August 1979, Def Leppard signed a record deal with Phonogram. The deal was rumored to be worth a million dollars, and the band became known as the first in the new wave of British heavy-metal bands to land such a lucrative contract.[10]

"We signed the record deal at Rick's parents' house," Elliott recalled, "because his dad had to sign for him because he was [only] 15."[11] The other band members were just a few years older.

Def Leppard started working on their major label debut while playing concerts. They were performing in front of larger crowds in better venues. For example, they opened for

Sammy Hagar at the Hammersmith Odeon in London. Hagar had been a member of the early American rock band Montrose before going out on his own. Later, he would join the very popular heavy-metal band Van Halen after that group parted ways with its lead singer, David Lee Roth. (Roth would eventually return to the group—and then leave again.) Def Leppard also opened for AC/DC, the pioneering heavy-metal band from Australia.

In March 1980, Def Leppard released *On Through the Night*. A few months later, the group traveled to the United States to tour the country for five months. They opened for established musicians Pat Travers, Judas Priest, and Ted

In 1979, Def Leppard signed a deal with Phonogram. From left to right: Joe Elliott, Rick Savage, Pete Willis, Rick Allen, and Steve Clark.

Nugent, among others. "Def Leppard looked good, sounded good and deserved the enthusiastic reception they received," one reviewer wrote after a concert in New York. "I'm sure the Big Apple will welcome another [performance] anytime in the future."[12]

The greetings the band received when they returned to their home country were less enthusiastic, however. Perhaps it was because one of the songs on the album was "Hello America." This was Def Leppard's first Top 50 hit; it reached number forty-five on the charts. Some music fans thought the song meant Def Leppard cared more about the United States than the United Kingdom, and that the band was selling out to attract American fans.

Elliott, who wrote "Hello America," said the song is about "a kid who . . . lives in Sheffield. . . . I didn't write it as a sellout song to gain popularity in America. When we first started out we knew we could get somewhere but it never entered my head it would get as far as entering the States. . . . It was just a song about me wanting to visit America and see all the places you see on the films."[13]

Def Leppard's first album had been a small success—but the group wanted more. In 1981, they began working on what would become their next album, *High 'n' Dry*. For this one, they called on the expertise of producer Robert John "Mutt" Lange. The members of Def Leppard believed that Lange would help them achieve the right sound: powerful and energetic but also melodious.

Lange already was a legend in the music business. He was not only a producer but also a sound engineer, musical arranger, singer, and songwriter. He had worked with the Boomtown Rats on their singles "Rat Trap" and "I Don't Like Mondays," which both hit number one in the United Kingdom. He also worked with AC/DC on their hit albums *Highway to Hell* and *Back in Black,* among others. In fact, Def Leppard had tried to hire Lange to work on their first album, but he had been unavailable. Lange would become so integral to Def Leppard's sound and success that the band members referred to him as the sixth member of the band.

On Through the Night had taken only eighteen days to record, but *High 'n' Dry* would take longer. Lange was a perfectionist who often rerecorded parts, and at one point, the band members wanted to take a break to watch soccer's World Cup series. When *High 'n' Dry* was finally released in July 1981, it did very well. The album became a Top 40 hit in Great Britain and went double platinum in the United States. This means that more than 2 million copies of the record were sold. Sales in the United States were helped by MTV, which played the video from "Bringin' on the Heartbreak" in heavy rotation. (This single was covered by Mariah Carey on her 2002 album *Charmbracelet.*)

Def Leppard toured throughout the United States and

Europe and the next year began working on a new album. Lange again was on board as producer. But although the band appeared to be strong, they were having problems. Guitarist Pete Willis was drinking heavily, and it was affecting his work in the studio. "Lange felt that a lot of the time Pete Willis wasn't responding to the things Lange asked him to do," Elliott said. "Willis had been having problems with his drinking for some time. . . . He was basically very shy, and drinking made it easier for him to get on stage and throw all of the right shapes. The problem was it also made him belligerent and argumentative."[14]

Willis's drinking was not the only issue; there were style conflicts as well. "Pete really wanted everybody to know what a great guitarist he was, not what a great songwriter he was," Elliott said. "So consequently, we had all these really difficult riffs" that even guitarist Steve Clark could barely follow. "That's all well and good, but it was detrimental to the song and detrimental to the furthering of the band," Elliott added, noting that Deep Purple's "Smoke on the Water" is "pretty simple to play and it's the most memorable song. Things didn't have to be so bloody complicated."[15]

In July 1982, the band members met without Willis and decided it was time to fire him. They arranged to meet him at the London home of their manager, Peter Mensch. Elliott called Willis before the meeting to let him know what was about to happen. "He was nice about it," Willis recalled. "He said, 'I'm really sorry, Pete, I didn't want to have to be the one to tell you this, but I got the job anyway.' After he said that, I knew what was coming next. I said I wanted to . . . talk about it. I didn't want to change their minds as much as to ask them why—although deep down, I knew why."[16]

"I felt really strange," Willis added. "One minute you're in a band that are set to conquer the world and . . . the next you're sitting at home twiddling your thumbs not knowing what to do. It was very disheartening."[17]

The remaining Def Leppard members were more optimistic about their future, however. They already knew who would replace Willis: Phil Collen. The guitarist was a longtime friend of the group and was part of a popular glitter-rock group called Girl.

"We'd known Phil for ages," Elliott said. "We always got on with him and he used to come by a lot and say hello. We always kept in touch and had respected him as a guitarist. He was the logical person to ask because he was a friend. We knew he would work hard. Also he looked good. He's got the right look for our group."[18]

Def Leppard's new album, *Pyromania,* was released in 1983. Willis was credited on the album, but a photo of him was not included. Collen did not write any of the songs, but he contributed key guitar solos and also played some rhythm guitar. More importantly, he brought a "completely fresh attitude," as Clark said. "He was excited about working and his attitude rubbed off on everyone else in the band."[19] Clark and Collen quickly became legendary guitar partners and friends offstage as well.

Pyromania featured layered vocal harmonies and heavy guitar riffs, a sound Def Leppard came to be known for. The album was a huge success, reaching number two on the U.S. charts. It was second only to Michael Jackson's *Thriller*. *Pyromania* sold so many copies that it was certified as diamond-selling, which means it sold more than 10 million copies. That is a rare achievement in the music business. Top songs from the album were "Photograph," which became the top-requested MTV video clip; "Rock of Ages"; and "Foolin'."

Once again, the band supported their album with touring. But for the first time, Def Leppard would be the headliner, not the warm-up act. To celebrate, the band members flew their parents to Los Angeles to attend two concerts there. The older generation knew their sons were successful musicians, but they had no idea of the scope until they attended the sold-out shows. "We had a great time," Collen said. "It freaked out our parents. My mum had never been out of England."[20]

American fans reported that they liked the musicians' looks, musicianship, attitude, and even the British flags on their shirts and shorts. "Def Leppard is, for sure, really hot," said one fan who attended the California concerts.[21] When the band played in Omaha, Nebraska, they recorded a public service announcement against arson at the request of the fire department chief. The word *pyromania* means "an obsession with fires and explosives," and the chief was worried that the popularity of the album would influence kids to start fires.

Def Leppard wrapped up their *Pyromania* tour in February 1984 in Thailand. The band not only survived the dismissal of a founding member but also had a huge success with their latest album. As the bandmates prepared to work on another new album, they had no idea they were about to enter a dark period in their history.

From the beginning, the making of *Hysteria* seemed to be jinxed. The band members did not have producer Lange at their side, and they did not agree with the direction in which the new producer wanted to take them. Then came drummer Rick Allen's car accident on New Year's Eve day in 1984. "It really was very traumatic," said Elliott of Allen's accident. "It seemed worse than death at the time."[22]

Allen spent four weeks in the hospital, and several more weeks recuperating at his parents' home in Sheffield. That terrible car crash changed his life completely, but he insisted the accident was not a tragedy. "It's the exact opposite," he said. "What I've experienced through losing my arm, I wouldn't change. The human spirit is so strong. When pushed, you either sink or swim. It is a choice."[23]

Allen chose to "swim." One day while lying in his hospital bed, he realized, "I could play all the basic patterns I originally played with both my arms with two feet."[24] Allen's friend

Peter Hartley, who experimented with electronics, was visiting at the time. He saw Allen moving his feet and realized what he was doing. Hartley offered to make Allen an electronic drum kit with custom pedals and drum pads. Electronic drums were rare at the time but are now more common.

After Allen left the hospital, he painstakingly learned to play drums again with his custom-built electronic drum kit. Meanwhile, the band tried recording with some of the tracks Allen had completed before the accident. They were not happy with the results, however. By the summer, producer Lange's schedule had eased. He began stopping by the studio to offer advice. Eventually, "he just kinda moved in," Savage said.[25] He told the band that everything needed to be rerecorded, and he also wrote some songs.

Lange was back on board, but the drama continued. During one recording session, Elliott lost his voice. Then he got the mumps and had to be hospitalized. Mumps is a disease caused by a virus that causes the glands to become painfully swollen. Elliott got better, but recording was delayed again when Lange broke his kneecap in a car accident. "It was like 'What . . . else can go wrong?'" Elliott said. "Bad luck's bad luck, but nobody deserves this much."[26]

Finally, in August 1987, *Hysteria* was released. It had been four years in the making, but all the work paid off. The album sold more than 16 million copies, launching Def Leppard into the exclusive group of bands with more than one diamond-selling album. (Only five other rock bands have two or more diamond records.) The album produced seven U.S. chart singles, including "Love Bites," "Pour Some Sugar on Me," and "Armageddon It."

"Pour Some Sugar on Me" was especially popular—and it almost was not written. During a recording session one day, Lange left the control room for a few minutes. While he was gone, Elliott picked up a guitar and started playing around on it. Lange returned in time to hear what Elliott was playing, and asked him what it was. "That's the best . . . hook I've heard in five years," Lange said. The hook became the chorus of "Sugar." "It became the most important song on the record," Elliott says. "And it was done almost by accident."[27]

Years later, country star Tim McGraw told *People Weekly* that "Pour Some Sugar on Me" was his secret rock-out song. "I like to get in my wife's [country singer Faith Hill] high heels and dance," he said.[28]

Not all the *Hysteria* reviews were glowing, however. One music critic called it a "pleasant record, much more consistent and polished [than *Pyromania*]. In other words, considering the kind of music they're supposed to be creating, it's a disappointment. . . . The boys are off the beam from the opening notes."[29]

Def Leppard spent most of 1988 on the road and played more than two hundred concert dates. They played many of their concerts on a round stage that included a spectacular

Def Leppard joined the many bands that became popular in the 1980s with big hair and colorful clothing.

light show. At first, the band hired another drummer to help Allen out. But when the drummer accidentally missed a gig, Allen proved he could do fine on his own. "There are at least half a dozen heartwarming rock and roll stories," said one concert reviewer. Allen's comeback "is one of them."[30]

The band members were feeling strong. "We've grown up a lot in the last four years," Elliott said. "Nothing seems like a big problem anymore. Jeez, if we can play with a one-armed drummer, we can do anything."[31] But soon, the band members would be tested once again.

In 1989, the Def Leppard bandmates turned their attention to making a new album. They were working without producer Lange, who decided to work with other performing artists. (One of those artists was country singer Shania Twain, whom Lange married in 1993. They separated in 2008.) For the most part, the band also was working without the help of guitarist Steve Clark. Like fellow founding member Pete Willis, Clark was having problems with alcohol.

Collen, too, had been an avid partier, but in the mid-1980s, he gave up drinking and became a vegan. To be vegan means to not eat meat, eggs, or dairy products. The group hired a special chef to cook for them during tours, and Collen persuaded others in the band to try the vegan lifestyle. Collen said his healthy living not only helped him personally but also professionally. "I feel so much better," Collen said. "I sing better and I play better."[32]

Clark, however, the other "terror twin," continued to drink, and his drinking began to affect his work. Throughout the years, Clark had been in and out of rehabilitation centers in an effort to overcome his addiction. He was never able to quit for long. Now, he was not contributing to the new album, and his bandmates were frustrated and worried. Finally, in September 1990, Clark's bandmates told him to take a six-month leave of absence from the group. They wanted him to

IN 1989, DEF LEPPARD PERFORMED ON A BRITISH TV SHOW CALLED *TOP OF THE POPS*.

combat his problem so that he could return to the band. Def Leppard had achieved great success in the eleven years since landing their first record deal, and Clark had been there from the beginning. Clark's band members were very hopeful that he would rejoin them; after all, they needed him.

Sadly, Clark's return never happened. On January 8, 1991, Steve Clark was found dead in his home in London. He had accidentally overdosed on a combination of alcohol and prescription medications he had been taking for a back injury. He was thirty years old. "I was upset . . . [but] I was almost already mentally prepared for it," Elliott said. "I felt as if the guy I knew didn't really exist anymore. When Rick lost his arm that was different, that was out of the blue, but with Steve we could see it coming for some time."[33]

"As a musician, [Clark] had so much to offer, so much that he'll never have a chance to express now," Elliott said. "I believe that if you've got it, flaunt it. And he had it."[34]

The remaining members of Def Leppard thought about disbanding. "I don't know what we're gonna do," Elliott said. "We have to get together and have a serious think about it. I must add, though, that it would be a shame if we did split up. The four of us still have a lot to offer, and I know the songs on this album are great. And Steve would be annoyed with us if we split up. . . . He'd say, '. . . Guys, get on with it!'"[35]

Ultimately, the band decided to stay together and complete the album without replacing Clark. Collen played all the guitar parts. In March 1992, *Adrenalize* was released; it was dedicated to Clark. The album entered the U.S. charts at number one and sold 6 million copies. The album also became the biggest-selling Def Leppard album in Japan and Mexico, among other countries. The album included a song called "White Lightning" that was written about Clark. That was another nickname for Clark because he frequently wore all-white clothing in concerts, running all around the stage as he played his guitar.

The month after *Adrenalize* was released, Def Leppard performed in a tribute concert to Queen lead singer Freddie Mercury, who had died the previous fall from complications of acquired immunodeficiency syndrome (AIDS). On the Wembley Stadium stage in London, the band members announced they had a new guitarist. Vivian Campbell, formerly of the bands Dio and Whitesnake, was joining Def Leppard as Clark's replacement.

Def Leppard spent most of 1993 touring to support *Adrenalize*. They played almost two hundred fifty shows around the world. Their schedule included the first concert in a newly built stadium in Sheffield, the band's hometown. The sellout crowd of forty thousand proved that after almost fifteen years in the music business, Def Leppard had finally gained respect in their home country.

The band also released an album featuring remixes of songs to which Clark had contributed. *Retro Active* went

Meet Vivian Campbell

The newest member of Def Leppard is Vivian Campbell, who joined the group in 1992 after the death of founding member Steve Clark.

Unlike the rest of his bandmates, Campbell is not an Englishman. Vivian Patrick Campbell was born on August 25, 1962, in Belfast, Northern Ireland. He began playing the guitar when he was twelve years old. Four years later, he dropped out of school to join the hard-core band Sweet Savage. The band toured Britain as the warm-up act for Thin Lizzy and Motorhead, and Sweet Savage released several singles. One of their songs was later covered by Metallica.

In 1983, Campbell left Sweet Savage to join the heavy-metal band Dio. He was with that group for four years before creative tensions inspired him to leave and join Whitesnake, another heavy-metal band. Whitesnake was a well-established band, but it had been having many problems and would soon break up. Campbell left the group after their 1988 world tour. He was working on a solo album when he got the call from Def Leppard lead singer Joe Elliott.

"Always having been a fan of Def Leppard's soaring harmonies and sterling pop hooks, it was a crossroads decision," Campbell wrote on his Web site. "You only get one chance to join a legendary rock band, and the solo album was put on hold."[36]

THE
FREDDIE MERCURY
TRIBUTE

SOLD OUT
THANK YOU ALL

CONCERT FOR AIDS AWARENESS
Profits to Aids Charities Worldwide

EASTER MONDAY APRIL 20th 1992
WEMBLEY STADIUM

Gates open 3.30pm   Show starts 6.00pm   Show finishes approx. 9.00pm

General Admission £25
A limited number of Reserved Seats at £30 and £35 available only by calling 081 862 0202

Personal callers welcome at Wembley Box Office and at Virgin Megastore Oxford St. & Marble Arch
also Allders of Croydon, Allders of Sutton, Bentalls of Kingston, and all branches of Keith Prowse

CREDIT CARD HOTLINES
Wembley Stadium 081 900 1234 / 071 240 7200 / 071 379 6131 / 071 836 4114
071 734 8932 / 071 580 3141

Limit of 6 tickets per person
(All tickets subject to booking fee except for personal callers at Wembley Box Office)
INFORMATION LINE (0891) 500 255 (calls charged at 36p cheap rate, 48p other times)

Concert produced by Queen and Harvey Goldsmith Entertainments   © 1992 Queen Productions Ltd.

In 1992, a month after their album *Adrenalize* was released, Def Leppard performed in a tribute concert to Queen lead singer Freddie Mercury.

platinum in the United States. Worldwide, more than 2 million copies were sold. The album also included a cover of the Bad Company song, "Miss You in a Heartbeat." The Def Leppard version landed in the Top 40.

In September 1993, Def Leppard played their final gig on the *Adrenalize* tour. The members decided to take a six-month break before beginning work on a new album. In the past several years, Def Leppard's career had skyrocketed. *Adrenalize* was selling well, but it was not as popular as the band's two previous albums had been. Musical tastes where changing; "grunge" had hit the scene. Could Def Leppard continue to attract fans, or was the band's heyday over?

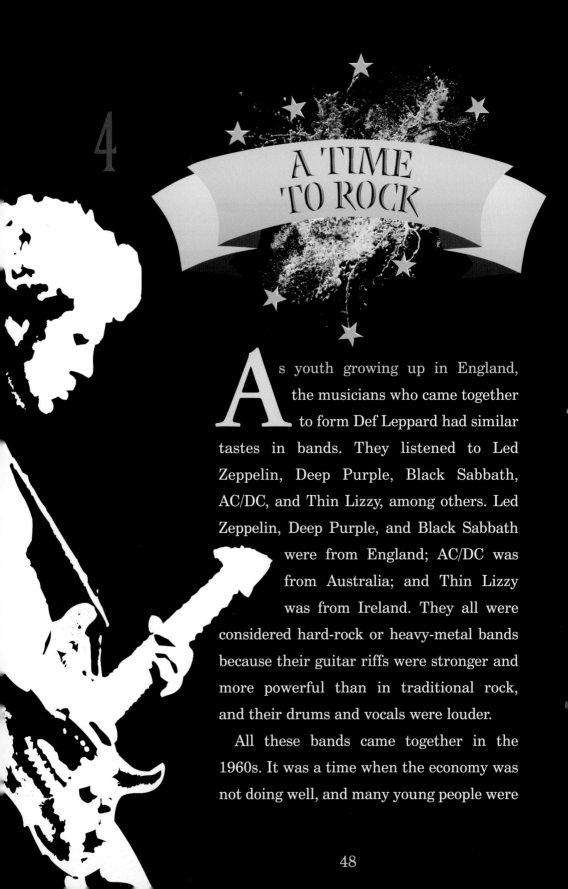

A TIME TO ROCK

4

As youth growing up in England, the musicians who came together to form Def Leppard had similar tastes in bands. They listened to Led Zeppelin, Deep Purple, Black Sabbath, AC/DC, and Thin Lizzy, among others. Led Zeppelin, Deep Purple, and Black Sabbath were from England; AC/DC was from Australia; and Thin Lizzy was from Ireland. They all were considered hard-rock or heavy-metal bands because their guitar riffs were stronger and more powerful than in traditional rock, and their drums and vocals were louder.

All these bands came together in the 1960s. It was a time when the economy was not doing well, and many young people were in low-paying jobs and feeling pessimistic about the future. There was also suspicion and distrust of authority figures. This atmosphere also gave rise in the mid-1970s to a genre of music called punk rock. Punk rock was characterized by short songs with spare use of instruments and angry, defiant lyrics.

"Punk was the rage in England" when Def Leppard came out, said guitarist Rick Savage. "Most club owners didn't want anything to do with a hard rock band. They wanted us to cut our hair and wear ripped t-shirts."[1]

Def Leppard certainly was not punk rock; the band members had even changed the spelling of their name so as to not cause any confusion. Def Leppard lead singer Joe Elliott once described punk rock as "heavy metal with singers who couldn't sing and guitar players who couldn't solo."[2]

Def Leppard was labeled a heavy-metal band, but that was not quite accurate, either. "We're really not a heavy metal band," the late Def Leppard guitarist Steve Clark once said. "I mean, we read. We can think."[3]

"The early heavy metal bands were much more menacing," according to Billy Warden, a former newspaper music critic who also has produced shows for E! Entertainment Network. "They were much more about creating a sense of menace, creating a sense that all was not right with the world, certainly that going out and having a party would not make things right with the world."[4]

Elliott said the early heavy-metal bands did influence Def

LED ZEPPELIN (FROM LEFT TO RIGHT: JOHN PAUL JONES, ROBERT PLANT, AND JIMMY PAGE. JOHN BONHAM IS PLAYING DRUMS.) WAS A BIG INFLUENCE ON THE MEMBERS OF DEF LEPPARD.

Leppard. But so, too, did musical groups that were known for their excellent melodies and lyrics. Def Leppard's first album, *On Through the Night,* was "full of harmonies that were more Queen and Beach Boys than just the obligatory vocals over a riff," Elliott said.[5]

"We just want to keep the guitars raunchy and still be melodic," Elliott said.[6] He added, "I like to think that we're actually a 'light alloy' band rather than heavy metal. We may have some of the same structures as metal, but we're very concerned with melody as well. That's something that separates us from most of the true metal bands."[7] Elliott said the label he prefers for Def Leppard is "hard rock, or just rock & roll."[8]

Don Tanner is a former radio disc jockey who wrote a book about radio called *No Static at All*. He said Def Leppard's music "rocked out, but the lyrics and melodies weren't traditionally what hard rock was about."[9]

"Heavy metal has always had sort of an underrated sense of melody about it," Warden said. Def Leppard, however, "brought the pop element to the fore. So they really made the hooks. Hooks are what makes the song catchy."[10] Before Def Leppard, Warden said, "hooks had not been associated with heavy metal. Def Leppard really brought that pop element into heavy metal."[11]

"I think it's absolutely fair to say that Def Leppard is a pop band more than anything else," said guitarist Vivian Campbell, the newest member of the group.[12]

In August 1981, Warner Communications launched Music Television, or MTV, a cable channel headquartered in New York City. The purpose of MTV was to broadcast music videos and provide news and information about performing artists. Never before had there been a television channel devoted solely to musicians and their works.

The influence of MTV was enormous on the bands whose

videos were played in heavy rotation. Sales for the Def Leppard album *High 'n' Dry* were average until MTV began airing the band's video for the song "Bringin' on the Heartbreak." The video was simply footage of Def Leppard performing the song on the stage of the Royal Court Theater in London. "MTV played it and the record went back up the charts," Clark said. "It was unbelievable."[13]

Def Leppard was the perfect band for MTV, Warden said. "They were young, they were fresh-faced, they were extremely energetic. They did fun, slightly goofy things like wear those shorts" with the British flag on them. "So they just came across with a great deal of energy, like a bunch of guys who had fun together, who had something to say together, and who you'd like to hang out with."[14]

Tanner said Def Leppard "was perceived as sounding different, coming around at a good time when people wanted to hear something different, and they rocked out but they were melodic at the same time."[15]

When MTV began, many homes did not yet have cable television. So in 1983, NBC launched a program called Friday Night Videos. The major television network wanted to compete against MTV, but the result was that bands got even more exposure. MTV, in a counterprogramming move, began airing Friday Night Video Fights, where viewers called in with their favorite videos. In 1983, Def Leppard's video for the single "Photograph," from the *Pyromania* album, was number one for twelve weeks. It beat out competitors including Duran Duran's "Hungry like the Wolf," Michael Jackson's "Beat It," and David Bowie's "China Girl."[16]

As exposure to musical groups and their songs increased, so, too, did parental concern about sexual and violent language in popular music. In 1985, the Parents' Music Resource Center (PMRC) was established. One of the group's founders was Tipper Gore. Her husband, Al, would later become the vice president of the United States. At the time, he was a Democratic senator from Tennessee. Gore said she was moved to action after she overhead the lyrics to a song by pop musician Prince on a record belonging to her daughter Karenna.[17]

The PMRC called on record companies to voluntarily issue warning labels on records that contained violent or sexually explicit material. The group also released the "Filthy Fifteen," a list of songs they found most objectionable. Def Leppard's "High 'n' Dry (Saturday Night)" made the list because of references to drug and alcohol use.

Party songs were "part of the entertainment," Elliott said. "The kids like us to do that. We like to do it as well, but we *don't* write about it all the time. And a lot of people seem to think that that's *it,* that we don't have opinions on anything else."[18]

When the Senate held a hearing on record labeling, Senator Paula Hawkins, a Republican from Florida, presented three album covers as offensive. She included Def Leppard's

Joe Elliott performing onstage in 1983

Pyromania because the cover image was a building with flames shooting out of it. An outline of a target is superimposed over the flames. Hawkins interpreted the cover as glorifying violence.

The PMRC had a lot of public support, and many record companies agreed to carry the warning labels. The voluntary labeling system remains in place today. Wal-Mart and other stores have refused to sell albums that have labels, but many people believe the labels actually help sales. "All you've got to do is tell somebody this is a no-no and then that's what they want," said Philip Bailey, lead singer of the group Earth, Wind, and Fire.[19] One mother agreed with him. "I think it's like a status symbol to buy the CD because it has a warning on it," she said.[20]

In the mid-1990s, Def Leppard was competing for fans with other hard-rock or heavy-metal bands such as Aerosmith, Van Halen, and Bon Jovi. By the 1990s, however, many music fans were turning to grunge music. A combination of punk, heavy metal, and indie rock, the music usually includes heavily distorted electronic guitars and dark, depressing lyrics. Popular grunge bands included Pearl Jam and Nirvana.

Perhaps that is why *Adrenalize,* which came out in 1992, did not do as well as the two Def Leppard albums it followed. "We felt that we made slightly the wrong album with . . . *Adrenalize,*" Savage said. "It should have been less polished and just a little more aware of the year it was competing in."[21]

Tanner said sometimes, the success of a band is all in the timing. When Def Leppard began making records, "the tide was starting to turn away" from the kind of dance music that Prince and Michael Jackson were making, he said. "But it was before the grunge of Nirvana and Pearl Jam. So part of [Def Leppard's success]" was timing, he said.[22]

Rock and roll, hard rock, punk rock, heavy metal, grunge. In the 1990s, Def Leppard still had millions of fans. Musical tastes were changing, however, and the twenty-first century was on the horizon. What would the new millennium hold for Def Leppard?

WHAT THE FANS WANT

5

*A*drenalize sold about 3 million copies, even as sales of hard-rock and heavy-metal albums overall were slowing down. The album debuted at number one and included several hit singles, including "Let's Get Rocked" and "Have You Ever Needed Someone So Bad." Lead singer Joe Elliott described the songs as "shorter and more to the point" then the songs from *Hysteria*. "The last album, we tended to drag songs out," he said. "This one, there's a couple that are mid-tempo, there are a few ballads. But rockers are rockers. And the ones we . . . consider . . . more in the vein of 'Pour Some Sugar on Me' and 'Armageddon It' . . . aren't really fast, but they've got power."[1]

Retailers in the United States reported that when *Adrenalize* first came out, it was selling more copies than Bruce Springsteen's two new releases, *Human Touch* and *Lucky Town*. A spokeswoman for the United Kingdom's largest music retailer, Our Price, said, "Sales of the Springsteen albums were very strong during the first couple of days. However, we expect Def Leppard to be the biggest-selling album this week."[2]

The album was also well reviewed by the critics. "The band offers its trademark formula: a sonic avalanche of crunching power chords, rock-solid rhythms and surprisingly tuneful vocals," wrote one critic.[3] "New producer Mike Shipley doesn't have Lange's heavy touch for symphonic metal," wrote another reviewer. "But on *Adrenalize* he adds his own embellishments . . . *Adrenalize* is superior to . . . *Hysteria*."[4]

The band's concerts were also well attended. A reviewer at one gig wrote that the show was delayed by equipment problems, and lead singer Joe Elliott's voice was strained from a cold. Those factors "may have caused lesser bands to put on a half-hearted concert," she wrote. "But not Def Leppard."[5]

"The fans appreciated the band's efforts," she added. "That's partly because the members of Def Leppard still come across like working-class Joes, albeit rich ones. They understand their fans like few major acts do and give them what they want without ever seeming condescending or bored.

That may ultimately prove to be a bigger talent than their estimable musicianship."[6]

Billy Warden, the former radio disc jockey, remembers seeing Def Leppard at a concert in Virginia. "It was a total celebration," he said. "And the band just seemed to have so much fun."[7]

In 1995, Def Leppard released a greatest hits album called *Vault.* It included one song from *High 'n' Dry,* two from *Pyromania,* six songs from *Hysteria,* four from *Adrenalize,* and two from *Retro Active.* The album also featured a new song, "When Love and Hate Collide," which became the band's biggest hit in the United Kingdom. It landed at number two on the charts there.

On October 23, 1995, the band played three concerts on three continents in the same day. Def Leppard performed in Tangiers at 5 A.M., and then traveled to London in time for a midday performance. They reached Vancouver for a 9 P.M. show.

After winding up their latest tour, the members of Def Leppard returned to the studio to begin working on yet another album. This would be the first full album to feature guitarist Vivian Campbell. The band wanted to try something different, so they used a recording studio in Spain. They wrote songs ranging from acoustic to heavy metal. Drummer Rick Allen used a regular acoustic drum kit instead of the electronic version that he had used since losing his arm.

IN 1995, DEF LEPPARD PERFORMED THREE CONCERTS ON THREE CONTINENTS ON THE SAME DAY. HERE THEY ARE PLAYING IN TANGIERS.

"This album is different from anything we've ever done," Elliott said. "But it's not so much the sound as the energy."[8]

Guitarist Phil Collen described the songs as a mix of styles. "I don't think there's ever been such a wealth of music as there is at the moment," he said. "Some bands I don't think are that great, and others I think are fantastic. So what we've always tried to do is take a bit from everything. A bit of Salt-n-Pepa. A bit of Boys II Men. A bit of Red Hot Chili Peppers. Just mix it all up. That's kind of what we did here" with *Slang*, Collen added. "It's one thing to copy something that's contemporary. It's another thing to actually understand it.

That's what we've done. We try to understand the new music and get to like it."[9]

Slang was released in May 1996. There were some favorable reviews: "Def Lep's most stripped-down music since 1983's *Pyromania* still has enough hooks and high harmonies to keep '80s fans happy," wrote one critic.[10] Another critic noted its "impressively executed blend of psychedelic music and melancholy lyrics."[11] Yet the album did not sell well. In fact, *Vault,* the band's compilation of greatest hits, was selling better. *Slang* is "a great-sounding record," Campbell said. "But I think we lost the plot with regard to songwriting on that, and I don't think we should have jettisoned that high standard in favor of just trying to capture a vibe."[12]

When the band members started working on a new album in 1998, they returned to their familiar roots. "Larger-than-life rock 'n' roll is our signature, and we're actually quite proud of it," Elliott said. "If anything, our mistake was briefly venturing away from it."[13] Collen said, "The signal could not have been more clear. People have decided what they want from this band, and that's just fine with us."[14]

The band recorded their new album, *Euphoria,* in Joe's Garage, Elliott's home studio in Dublin, Ireland. Producer Mutt Lange returned to help the band with three songs. While Def Leppard was working on the album, the cable television channel VH1 broadcast an episode of *Behind the Music* that featured Def Leppard. The popular VH1 series focused on musicians and the highs and lows of their careers. (The first *Behind the Music* episode was about Milli Vanilli, the German pop and dance music duo who won a Grammy Award for Best New Artist in 1990. The duo was forced to give back their Grammy when it was learned that they did not do the singing on their album.)

Def Leppard released *Euphoria* in 1999. Guitarist Campbell described the album as, "Let's rip ourselves off and do a classic Leppard-sounding record with all the bells and whistles."[15] But although the record featured the band's signature sound, it sold only about 550,000 copies. The band toured through the United States and Canada to support the album. It was the first time in three years that Def Leppard had gone on the road. This time, many of their shows were played in smaller venues, such as state fairs and festivals. However, they found enthusiastic crowds at all their shows.

"I tried to [get] them for all of my fairs," said Dave Snowden, a promoter in Louisville, Kentucky. "To me, that show is the absolute find of the year. It's been strong out of the gate with very little advertising."[16] Another promoter, who booked Def Leppard for a fair in Michigan, said, "They are easy guys to work with, very professional, a delight."[17]

VH1 continued to air the Def Leppard episode of *Behind the Music* in reruns, and it was one of the most popular episodes of the series. VH1 produced three additional Def Leppard-related shows, including *Hysteria: The Def Leppard*

Story. This fictionalized story of the drama surrounding the making of the *Hysteria* album was broadcast in 2001. It featured the tag line: "Music made them legends. Tragedy made them heroes."

"A lot of younger people are discovering the band through things like *Behind the Music*," Campbell said.[18] But as Savage

IN 2001, A FICTIONALIZED STORY ABOUT DEF LEPPARD WAS PRODUCED BY VH1. THIS IS A STILL FROM THE FILM *HYSTERIA: THE DEF LEPPARD STORY*.

noted, "Unfortunately, the major talking point about our band is that there has been tragedy along the way. It does not mirror the way that we express ourselves in records, which we've always believed have got to be larger than life and fun and make people smile."[19]

The disappointing sales of *Euphoria* did not dissuade the band from putting out another album. *X,* like the Roman numeral for ten, to symbolize the band's tenth album, was released in July 2002. It was yet another Def Leppard album with weak sales. In fact, *X* did not even go gold. Yet Def Leppard proved they could still fill concert seats. The band played several shows in the United Kingdom, including one that was attended by Queen Elizabeth. They also traveled throughout Canada, Japan, the United States, Germany, Poland, Latvia, Lithuania, and Russia. In 2003, after more than one hundred fifty shows, Def Leppard ended the *X* tour in Moscow.

"There's really nothing in the world that can match the sensation of a curtain going up to reveal [thousands of] screaming people on their feet cheering you on," Elliott once said. "You feel an energy and a freedom that's just impossible to match in the studio."[20] In a live chat with *USA Today* subscribers, Elliott also said he did not like to sing "Photograph" anymore because "it's bloody hard! If you listen to that song, other than the guitar solo, there's no breathing room in that song. If you're not on the top of your game, it's like trying to ice skate on Mount Everest. I love the song, but I've done it since 1983."[21]

X proved to be Def Leppard's final album of new material to date. In 2004, the band released *Best of Def Leppard*. The next year, an updated version was released called *Rock of Ages—The Definitive Collection*. That same year, Def Leppard performed in Philadelphia as part of the Live 8 concerts. These concerts took place in ten cities around the globe and featured performances by the biggest names in the music industry. The purpose was to raise awareness of problems in Africa, including famine and poverty. Def Leppard also performed in 2005 on the popular late-night television show *Jimmy Kimmel Live* and at two major awards shows.

Def Leppard took to the road, too. The band toured through the United States as co-headliners with Bryan Adams. He is a Canadian-English singer-songwriter who has received Academy Award nominations for songs he wrote for major motion pictures.

The Def Leppard–Bryan Adams concerts took place in minor-league ballparks and were very popular, in large part because tickets and concessions were reasonably priced. "People are catching on that the shows are a great family experience at a great price," one tour promoter said.[22]

In 2005, guitarist Rick Savage talked about what it was like to no longer be at the top of the charts and to be playing in smaller venues. "We took it in stride because music needs to progress," he said. "The only disappointing thing was that a lot of the grunge bands that came after could only create an identity by stating that they were anti-Def Leppard, rather than going on the positive and proclaiming what was great about their own band."[23]

Savage also noted that Def Leppard was still around, while other bands of various genres had long broken up. "In any successful musical movement, there are always two or three bands that either started it, or were at the pinnacle in that era. Those bands survive because they are the genuine articles."[24]

In 2006, Def Leppard released an album called *Yeah!* All the songs were covers of the band's favorite tunes, including Free's 1972 "Little Bit of Love," Badfinger's 1970 "No Matter What," David Essex's "Rock On" from 1973, and the Kinks' "Waterloo Sunset," from 1967.

"I thought it was about time we showed the world what our true [musical] roots were," Elliott said. "The songs on this album are at least partly responsible for us making the kind of music that we do."[25] Collen said, "We didn't want to make the standard covers album and gave this a lot of deep thought as Joe has been going on about doing this sort of project for 26 years. We wanted to express ourselves through these songs and approached the recording process as if they were our own."[26]

The release received some mixed reviews. One critic

wrote, "Talk about peculiar. . . . It's odd to hear one of Britain's greatest metal bands" perform some of the songs. "The interpretation is solid, but you wouldn't know you were listening to [Def Leppard] 'til the guitars kick in."[27]

However, other critics liked it, and the band appeared on *The Tonight Show with Jay Leno* and *Live with Regis & Kelly.*

To support the album, the band toured through Italy, Sweden, Germany, Holland, and the United Kingdom. They also teamed with Journey for a co-headlining tour of North America. Journey is an American rock band that was popular in the late 1970s and early 1980s for its power ballads.

An Extreme Fan

It is one thing to really like a band's music. It is another thing to take that feeling to an extreme. In November 1993, National Public Radio reported the story of a radio disc jockey in Beaver Falls, Pennsylvania, who became so tired of the light rock his station required him to play that one day, he nailed shut the door to his studio and played Def Leppard's "Rock! Rock! Till You Drop," from the band's 1983 *Pyromania* album, for more than twenty hours. The disc jockey was fired.

The Def Leppard–Journey summer tour proved to be one of the biggest-selling concert tours of the year. Many gigs were sold out, and the tour was extended through the fall to accommodate fans who were not able to land tickets to previous gigs. "We know that the Rolling Stones, Kenny Chesney, Tim McGraw/Faith Hill, and Dave Matthews Band will sell the heck out of tickets" when they tour, wrote music critic Ray Waddell in *Billboard* magazine. "But there is always a dark horse that rises seemingly out of nowhere to become a huge seller each year. . . . [In 2006] it was the Def Leppard/Journey package."[28]

"Both bands put on great shows," one reviewer wrote. "The crowd was a testament to that. If you looked around, you saw all ages, from kids to folks who must have been in their late 40s. Good showmanship, an arsenal of recognizable songs and strong musicianship always attracts a huge crowd. The allure's a no-brainer. . . . Def Leppard and Journey delivered fist-pumping, sing-till-you're-hoarse material."[29]

Another reviewer wrote, "The fans, from teens to couples with their kids, still sang along to every word . . . like it was 1984 all over again. . . . The reason for this concert's success was that both bands played their sizable catalog of hits with verve and brisk enthusiasm."[30]

"This tour is a classic example of the phrase one plus one equals three," said Adam Kornfeld, who helped put the tour together. "A package like this is a guaranteed night of hits,

Catch the References

Some of Def Leppard's greatest hits are more than thirty years old, but the band's influence can still be seen in pop culture. In an episode of the NBC television comedy *My Name Is Earl* that was broadcast in 2006, the character Earl mentioned Def Leppard. Also, in the 2007 major motion picture comedy *Balls of Fury*, the main character, a Ping-Pong prodigy, wears a Def Leppard shirt with his short shorts and silvery jacket. The movie also included versions of the Def Leppard songs "Rock of Ages," "Pour Some Sugar on Me," and "Photograph."

memories, fun and showmanship."[31] Def Leppard also released a DVD in 2006 called *Rock of Ages: The Definitive Collection*. It sold briskly and reached number fifteen on the list of top-selling music videos for 2006.

Lead singer Joe Elliott once said that while the band enjoyed touring and playing their hit songs, "One thing this band will never be is a nostalgia band. . . . We're not old enough to retire," he said, "and we feel young enough to keep wanting to do it . . . and we're 20 years younger" than the Rolling Stones.[32] That English rock band, which formed in the early 1960s, is still going strong today, churning out new material and drawing huge crowds to their concerts.

Def Leppard's recent concert successes proved the band could still draw fans. The band members were earning good money playing their old hits. However, the fans who flocked to their concerts were not buying the compact discs featuring new Def Leppard songs. Sales of the band's more recent CDs of new material had floundered. It looked as though Def Leppard had finally reached the point that creatively, the best days of the band were behind them.

"STILL ON TOP OF THEIR GAME"

More than three decades ago, five teenaged boys from Sheffield, England, got together to form a band. The lineup has changed a little—one founding member was fired, and another died before his time—but the music lives on.

Pete Willis, the guitarist who was fired from Def Leppard, went on to work with two other musical groups. Gogmagog was a band that included former musicians from the heavy-metal bands Iron Maiden and Whitesnake. The group released a three-song album in the mid-1980s but then disbanded. A few years later, Willis was part of a band called Roadhouse. The group released an album

71

in 1991 and went out on tour, but they did not find long-lasting success.

Today, Willis is out of the music business, though he joined Atomic Mass for a reunion concert in 2003. He lives in Sheffield, where he and his wife have their own property-management company.

Drummer Rick Allen had some anger-management issues in the years following his crash. In 1996, he pleaded guilty to assaulting his then-wife and was ordered to make public service announcements to air on MTV. Allen grew interested in spirituality and healing energy, and in 2001 he established the Raven Foundation. The goal of this nonprofit group is to help people who have experienced trauma heal through arts programs, such as drumming workshops.

"Typically, what that involves is breathing exercises, visualization, meditation, and drumming," Allen said. He described one visit to a teen cancer center in Sheffield as "an empowering experience [that] took [the patients] away from the difficulties they were experiencing in treatment, and ultimately . . . they experienced a sense of community and that they weren't alone."[1]

"Our mission is to celebrate diversity and bring people together through their common beliefs," Allen also said. "And love is the most basic way that we are all brought together as one family."[2]

Through the Raven Foundation, Allen has helped military

IN 2007, RICK ALLEN LED A DRUM CIRCLE DURING A RAVEN FOUNDATION EVENT.

veterans, children with cancer, and Hurricane Katrina survivors, among others. He finds his work very gratifying, particularly when he works with kids. "I know how bad I felt at the worst times," he said. "Sometimes just going out and being with people in that situation is all they need. They look at me and say he's one of us."[3]

Allen admits that sometimes his disability can be frustrating, "but as we all know, life is a constant learning curve," he said. "So, I turn my frustration into action and try to improve on what I've been blessed with."[4]

"I think I feel more complete now than I ever did," Allen said. "It puts all your priorities into perspective. It has for me, anyway. All those stupid thoughts that come into your mind they don't anymore. I seem to be able to command a situation better."[5]

Allen has two children. He lives in Malibu, California, with his second wife, Lauren Monroe, who started the Raven Foundation with him.

Guitarist Phil Collen lives with his wife and two children in California. With Def Leppard bandmate Joe Elliott, he formed a band called Cybernauts. They play covers of David Bowie songs and have released a CD. Collen also started a three-piece alternative-rock band called Man-Raze. The group plans to release a CD one day.

In 2007, Collen finally indulged a childhood dream and bought an Aston Martin, which is a British luxury car. "I've wanted it since I was 7," he said. "I remember I saw James Bond and I said, 'I want that car!' And now I finally got around to getting it. I mean, it's so ridiculously overpriced, really. But it's still cool."[6]

Guitarist Rick Savage is married and has two sons. Like the other Def Leppard members, Savage is an avid soccer fan. In fact, Def Leppard once played a soccer match against the members of Iron Maiden, another English heavy-metal band. Savage and the other members of Def Leppard also like to play golf while on tour. Savage also enjoys restoring and redecorating houses.

Savage lives with a condition called Bell's palsy. This is when the muscles in the face become paralyzed. Savage first contracted Bell's palsy in the 1990s and has largely recovered from it, but it flares up every once in a while.

Guitarist Vivian Campbell lives in California with his wife and two daughters. He regularly plays soccer with Hollywood United Football Club, a team of celebrities and former professional athletes. (Soccer is called football in many countries around the world.) Campbell has now been with Def Leppard longer than Clark was, and he finally finished the solo album he was working on when he got the call to join the heavy-metal group. *Two Sides of If* was released in 2005. Campbell not only plays guitar on the blues-based album but also sings.

"The Leppard vocal strength [is] something that we all pride ourselves on and work hard to maintain," he said. "We warm up before every performance using a technique that my vocal coach . . . taught the band . . . after I had joined for the 'Adrenalize' tour. We frequently have people ask us if we're using vocal samples or backing tapes in our live performances and, frankly, we'll take that as a compliment."[7]

Lead singer Joe Elliott has been married twice and has no children. He lives in Dublin, Ireland, where he has his own recording studio. Aside from his work with Def Leppard and

Cybernauts, Elliott has been involved in independent projects. He contributed to a tribute album to American shock rocker Alice Cooper. He also helped Rolling Stones guitarist Ronnie Wood on his solo album, among other projects.

Def Leppard has sold more than 65 million records and has played in concerts all over the world. The band's 1983 album, *Pyromania,* was included on *Rolling Stone* magazine's list of the five hundred greatest albums of all time. The album that followed four years later, *Hysteria,* is one of the top-selling albums ever. In fact, only six albums in history have sold more copies. *Hysteria* and *Pyromania* also received diamond awards for sales above 10 million, a feat few bands have achieved. *Vault,* the 1995 collection of greatest hits, has sold more than 7 million copies.

Elliott is proud of what Def Leppard has accomplished. "We always tried to make records that would sound good in a live environment," he said. "Of course, being from Sheffield, it was either this or work in a factory until we're 65."[8] Elliott also said, "I told my [high school] careers officer I was going to be a rock star or a footballer," the British term for soccer player, "and I wasn't that great at football. I love being a rock star on stage, but otherwise, people can come and talk to me, I'm approachable. . . . I'm the one in 10 million" who had his dream come true.[9]

While Def Leppard's classic recordings have impressive sales figures, newer releases have not done as well. However, the band continues to draw old fans, and even attract younger generations of fans, with their lively, energetic stage shows featuring their hits from decades past. The band's tour with Journey in the summer of 2006 grossed more than $35 million. "Don't even think . . . Def Leppard [is] no longer viable . . . because a sold-out crowd . . . outside of Houston would prove you wrong," one music critic wrote. He said the band delivered a "night full of hits that made the standing room only crowd flick their Bics and scream like teenagers all over again."[10] Another critic wrote that the band members were "tight players who are still on top of their game decades after they peaked."[11]

"Def Leppard is consistently one of the most exciting and successful bands we work with year in and year out," one tour promoter said. "There is no better way to kick off our touring season than with Def Leppard."[12]

Collen once was asked why he thought the band was so successful. "We don't take it all too seriously," he said. "When our success began in the States we took it with a pinch of salt because you see so many bands who have a bit of success and then nothing."[13]

"With us it's been a combination of lots of different things," Collen added. "I think the most important thing has been the way we've worked hard and the attitude of the band. We don't have ego problems and our image has helped."[14] "We're ordinary and normal," he also said. "We try to avoid

In 2008, Def Leppard released a new album—*Songs From the Sparkle Lounge.*

limos when we can. Some people know our drummer has got one arm, but apart from that it's just, like, five guys."[15]

And of course, there is the music. Def Leppard songs are "good songs," said Don Tanner, the former disc jockey and author of *No Static at All*. "It's good music, it's really good music, really good melodies," he said. "It's catchy and up tempo. When you listen to their music again, I don't think it got burned out, like some records may have. And people like to hear that again. It does stand the test of time, I think their music really does. It's good stuff."[16] Billy Warden, another former disc jockey, agreed that Def Leppard's songs have held up well after all these years. "When you hear 'Photograph,' or 'Pour Some Sugar on Me'—those are great songs," he said. "They're going to sound great twenty-five years from now."[17]

Warden added that "Pour Some Sugar on Me" "was just huge. I mean, it's hard to really put across what that sounded like on the radio back in 1987. It was so—an instant party of a song, and really well made."[18]

Though the Def Leppard bandmates have been involved in independent projects as well as their families, they come together for concert tours. Def Leppard performed fifty concerts in the summer of 2007, and they scheduled several concerts in North America for the spring of 2008. The group also released a new CD, *Songs From the Sparkle Lounge*. One of the songs features country singer Tim McGraw.

"There is a special bond between the five members of

DEF LEPPARD STILL PLAYS AND CONTINUES TO PRODUCE HIT ALBUMS.

Def Leppard, and there's a spark whenever we get together," said Savage. "It's like stepping into a time capsule, because the feeling is exactly the same as it was when we were teenagers. That's why we still enjoy what we do so much."[19]

No longer the teenage prodigy, Allen now has been playing drums longer with one arm than he played with two arms. He plays an acoustic-electric drum kit and said he is often asked why he smiles so much when he is drumming. His answer is that he not only enjoys what he is doing, but he is also at peace. Before every show, Allen says a prayer along the lines of "May this be good for everyone involved." "Something like that has the power to go a long way," Allen said.[20]

So all is well in Def Leppard's world, though the anniversary of guitarist Steve Clark's death remains difficult. "He could really fill the stage," Elliott said. "He used to do the Chuck Berry thing, strutting across the stage. And where Chuck Berry would do it at five miles an hour, Steve would do it ninety in reverse. You had to get out of his way or you were going to get knocked offstage."[21]

But if anyone still wants to call any aspect of the Def Leppard story "tragic," Savage had this to say: "We've lost a guitar player and a friend [Clark] and we nearly lost a friend and a drummer [Allen]. . . . But the story continues, and that in itself is a triumph."[22]

TIMELINE

1957—Phil Collen is born on December 8.

1959—Joe Elliott is born on August 1.

1960—Pete Willis is born on February 16; Steve Clark is born on April 23; Rick Savage is born on December 2.

1962—Vivian Campbell is born on August 25.

1963—Rick Allen is born on November 1.

1977—Willis and Savage form Atomic Mass, then meet Elliott and become Def Leppard.

1978—Steve Clark joins Def Leppard; the band plays its first gig in July; Rick Allen joins the band in November.

1979—*The Def Leppard EP,* recorded without Allen, is released in January; the band signs a record deal with Phonogram in August.

1980—The band releases its first major-label album, *On Through the Night,* in March.

1981—*High 'n' Dry* is released in July; Music Television channel (MTV) debuts in August.

1982—Guitarist Pete Willis is fired in July during the recording of *Pyromania* and is replaced by Phil Collen.

1983—*Pyromania* is released in February; it will reach number two on the U.S. charts, sell millions of copies, and be named one of the greatest rock albums ever.

1984—During the recording of *Hysteria,* drummer Rick Allen loses his arm in a car accident on New Year's Eve day.

1985—The Parents' Music Resource Center calls for warning labels on records that contain violent or sexually explicit material.

1987—The long-delayed *Hysteria* is released in August; it will go on to sell more than 16 million copies.

1989—Def Leppard starts work on their next album.

1991—Guitarist Steve Clark is found dead on January 8 from an accidental overdose of alcohol and prescription medications; the band decides to complete their next album as a foursome.

1992—*Adrenalize* is released in March; Vivian Campbell is announced as the newest band member in April.

1993—*Retro Active* is released in August.

1995—*Vault* is released in October; that same month, Def Leppard plays three concerts on three continents in the same day.

1996—*Slang* is released in May to favorable reviews but so-so sales.

1998—VH1 broadcasts the Def Leppard episode of its *Behind the Music* series.

1999—*Euphoria* is released in April.

2000—Def Leppard is inducted in the Hollywood RockWalk Hall of Fame in September.

2001—Allen forms the nonprofit Raven Foundation to help people who have experienced trauma. In July, VH1 broadcasts the fictionalized *Hysteria: The Def Leppard Story.*

2002—*X*, the band's tenth album, is released in July.

2004—*Best of Def Leppard* comes out in October.

2005—*Rock of Ages—The Definitive Collection* is released in May; Def Leppard performs in Philadelphia in July as part of the Live 8 concerts.

2006—The band releases the covers album *Yeah!* in May and has a very successful summer tour co-headlining with Journey.

2007—Def Leppard performs fifty summer concerts.

2008—*Songs From the Sparkle Lounge* is released.

DISCOGRAPHY

1979 *The Def Leppard EP*

1980 *On Through the Night*

1981 *High 'n' Dry*

1983 *Pyromania*

1987 *Hysteria*

1992 *Adrenalize*

1993 *Retro Active*

1995 *Vault*

1996 *Slang*

1999 *Euphoria*

2002 *X*

2004 *The Best of Def Leppard*

2005 *Rock of Ages—The Definitive Collection*

2006 *Yeah!*

2008 *Songs From the Sparkle Lounge*

CONCERT TOURS

1978–1979 Early Tours

1980 On Through the Night

1981 High 'n' Dry

1983 Pyromania

1987 Hysteria

1992 Adrenalize

1995 Vault (Promo Tour)

1996 Slang

1999 Euphoria

2002 X / Ten

2005 Rock of Ages

2006 YEAH!

2007 Downstage Thrust

2008 Songs From the Sparkle Lounge

GLOSSARY

acoustic—A musical instrument that has not been electronically modified.

avid—To be very enthusiastic about something.

fledgling—Something that is new or inexperienced.

flounder—To struggle to move or be effective.

gig—A job that will be performed for a short period of time.

harmony—The combination of simultaneous notes in a chord.

hook—A device to grab the attention of listeners.

integral—Something that is essential to completeness.

jam—To improvise while playing music with others.

jettison—To get rid of or forgo something.

lyrics—Words to a song.

marketing—Process of selling, promoting, or distributing a product or service.

mumps—A viral disease that causes the glands to become painfully swollen.

pyromania—An intense interest in fires and explosives.

riff—Rapid and often improvised series of notes.

sever—To become separated.

CHAPTER NOTES

Chapter 1. A Freak Accident

1. Chris Collingwood, *Def Leppard: No Safety Net* (Surrey, England: Castle Communications, 1994), p. 50.

2. Kurt Loder, "Def Leppard Drummer Loses Arm in Crash," *Rolling Stone*, February 14, 1985, p. 11.

3. David Fricke, *Def Leppard: Animal Instinct* (London, England: Zomba Books, 1987), p. 106.

4. Ibid., p. 8.

5. Ibid., p. 10.

6. Rob Tannenbaum, "Def Leppard Unleashes 'Hysteria,'" *Rolling Stone*, September 10, 1987, p. 16.

7. Fricke, p. 11.

8. Collingwood, p. 85.

9. Tom Kisken, "Beat of a Different Drum: Def Leppard's Rick Allen Lives in Rhythm, With One Arm and Heart," *Ventura County Star*, July 19, 2003, p. E4.

10. Luke Crampton and Dafydd Rees, *Rock & Roll Year by Year* (London, England: DK Publishing Inc., 2003), p. 385.

11. Collingwood, p. 85.

Chapter 2. The Def Leppard Lineup

1. Rob Richard, "Interview: Rick Allen of Def Leppard," *Handidrummed.com,* March 12, 2006, <http://www.handidrummed.com/interviews/rick_allen.php> (January 31, 2008).
2. Ibid.
3. Ibid.
4. Chris Crocker, *Monsters of Metal: Def Leppard, a Biography* (New York: Ballantine Books, 1986), p. 10.
5. Ibid., p. 20.
6. John Swenson, "Def Leppard Breaks the Heavy-metal Mold," *Rolling Stone,* October 2, 1980, p. 27.
7. David Fricke, *Def Leppard: Animal Instinct* (London, England: Zomba Books, 1987), p. 17.
8. Ibid.
9. Philip Anderson, "Joe Elliot—Singer, Def Leppard," *KAOS,* 2000, <http://www.kaos2000.net/interviews/defleppard/joeelliott00.html> (January 28, 2008).
10. Fricke, p. 75.
11. Crocker, p. 78.
12. David Fricke, "Def Leppard Guitarist Found Dead in London Home," *Rolling Stone,* February 21, 1991, p. 14.
13. Ibid.
14. Ibid.

Chapter 3. Hello America, Hello World

1. David Fricke, *Def Leppard: Animal Instinct* (London, England: Zomba Books, 1987), p. 19.

2. Chris Crocker, *Monsters of Metal: Def Leppard, a Biography* (New York: Ballantine Books, 1986), p. 42.

3. John Senson, "Def Leppard Breaks the Heavy-metal Mold," *Rolling Stone*, October 2, 1980, p. 27.

4. Crocker, p. 13.

5. Chris Collingwood, *Def Leppard: No Safety Net* (Surrey, England: Castle Communications, 1994), p. 17.

6. Fricke, p. 26.

7. Ibid., p. 29.

8. Philip Anderson, "Joe Elliot–Singer, Def Leppard," *KAOS*, 2000, <http://www.kaos2000.net/interviews/defleppard/joeelliott00.html> (January 28, 2008).

9. Chris Welch, *Def Leppard: Illustrated Biography* (London, England: Omnibus Press, 1984), p. 29.

10. Crocker, p. 32.

11. Anderson.

12. Welch, p. 42.

13. Ibid., p. 48.

14. Collingwood, p. 53.

15. Anderson.

16. Fricke, p. 75.

17. Collingwood, p. 60.

18. Welch, p. 54.

19. Crocker, p. 79.

20. Welch, p. 56.

21. Bruce D. Rhodewalt, "Def Leppard: Heavy Metal for People Who Think," *Rolling Stone,* July 7, 1983, p. 47.

22. Rob Tannenbaum, "Def Leppard Unleashes 'Hysteria,'" *Rolling Stone,* September 10, 1987, p. 16.

23. Ryan O'Quinn, "Def Leppard Drummer Inspires Many Through Local Foundation," *Malibu Times,* July 17, 2003, p. B12.

24. Kevin Stein, "Rick Takes the Driver's Seat in His Home Studio," *The Raven Drum Foundation,* September 2002, <http://www.ravendrumfoundation.org/interview_rick01.htm> (January 28, 2008).

25. Tannenbaum, p. 91.

26. Ibid.

27. Fred Goodman, et al., "The 25 Best-selling Albums of All Time," *Entertainment Weekly,* May 3, 1996, p. 24.

28. Danielle Anderson, "What's Your Secret Rock-Out Song? (Chatter)," *People Weekly,* February 7, 2005, p. 124.

29. David Hiltbrand, "Hysteria," *People Weekly,* September 28, 1987, p. 22.

30. Steve Dougherty, "Def Leppard Keeps Their One-armed Drummer and Turns Tragedy Into Hysteria," *People Weekly,* May 16, 1988, p. 89.

31. Ibid.

32. Amy Rosenbaum, "Heavy Metal Veggie," *Vegetarian Times,* March 1993, p. 132.

33. Collingwood, p. 113.

34. David Fricke, "Def Leppard Guitarist Found Dead in London Home," *Rolling Stone,* February 21, 1991, p. 14.

35. Ibid.

36. Vivian Campbell, n.d. <http://www.myspace.com/viviancampbell> (June 1, 2009).

Chapter 4. A Time to Rock

1. Chris Crocker, *Monsters of Metal: Def Leppard, a Biography* (New York: Ballantine Books, 1986), pp. 14–15.

2. Chris Welch, *Def Leppard: Illustrated Biography* (London, England: Omnibus Press, 1984), p. 80.

3. Steve Dougherty, "Def Leppard Keeps Their One-armed Drummer and Turns Tragedy Into Hysteria," *People Weekly,* May 16, 1988, p. 89.

4. Personal interview with Billy Warden, November 5, 2007.

5. Chris Willman, "Rock of Ages: Bonus Music

Section 2006: Listen to This," *Entertainment Weekly,* May 19, 2006, p. L2T6.

6. Welch, p. 80.

7. Crocker, pp. 68–69.

8. John Swenson, "Def Leppard Breaks the Heavy-metal Mold," *Rolling Stone,* October 2, 1980, p. 27.

9. Personal interview with Don Tanner, January 17, 2008.

10. Personal interview with Billy Warden, November 5, 2007.

11. Ibid.

12. Willman.

13. Crocker, p. 106.

14. Personal interview with Billy Warden, November 5, 2007.

15. Personal interview with Don Tanner, January 17, 2008.

16. Crocker, p. 107.

17. Laura S. Jeffrey, *Al Gore: Leader for the New Millennium* (Berkeley Heights, N.J.: Enslow Publishers, 1999), p. 40.

18. Bruce D. Rhodewalt, "Def Leppard: Heavy Metal for People Who Think," *Rolling Stone,* July 7, 1983, p. 43.

19. Peter Bowles, "Spotlight on Explicit Lyrics Warning," *BBC News,* May 27, 2002, <http://

news.bbc.co.uk/1/hi/entertainment/music/2010641. stm> (February 4, 2008).

20. Ibid.

21. Willman.

22. Personal interview with Don Tanner, January 17, 2008.

Chapter 5. What the Fans Want

1. David Fricke, "Def Leppard: Ready to Roar?" *Rolling Stone,* October 17, 1991, p. 24.

2. Paul Verna, Ed Christman, Jeff Clark-Meads, and Wolfgang Spahr, "Springsteen, Def Lep Race From Gate: Retailers Report Brisk Sales in U.S., Europe," *Billboard,* April 11, 1992, p. 7.

3. "Reviews: Thunder at the Top of the Charts," *Time,* April 20, 1992, p. 101.

4. David Hiltbrand, "Adrenalize," *People Weekly,* May 11, 1992, p. 22.

5. Melinda Newman, "Def Leppard," *Billboard,* August 29, 1992, p. 18.

6. Ibid.

7. Personal interview with Billy Warden, November 5, 2007.

8. Melinda Newman, "What I Did on My London 'Vacation': Radio Report; Def Leppard in the Studio," *Billboard,* March 11, 1995, p. 12.

9. Jeremy Helligar, "Talking With . . . Def

Leppard's Phil Collen: The Leppard Changes Its Spots," *People Weekly,* May 20, 1996, p. 27.

10. Chuck Eddy, "Slang," *Entertainment Weekly,* May 17, 1996, p. 62.

11. Larry Flick, "Def Leppard Delivers 'Euphoria,'" *Billboard,* May 15, 1999, p. 14.

12. Chris Willman, "Rock of Ages: Bonus Music Section 2006: Listen to This," *Entertainment Weekly,* May 19, 2006, p. L2T6.

13. Flick.

14. Ibid.

15. Willman.

16. Don Muret, "Def Leppard Returns to Concert Scene After Three-year Absence," *Amusement Business,* August 2, 1999, p. 5.

17. Ibid.

18. Willman.

19. Ibid.

20. Chris Crocker, *Monsters of Metal: Def Leppard, a Biography* (New York: Ballantine Books, 1986), pp. 111–112.

21. "VH1's Ultimate Albums: Pyromania': Def Leppard's Joe Elliott," *USA Today.com,* March 6, 2002, <http://www.usatoday.com/community/chat/2002-03-06-elliott.htm> (January 28, 2008).

22. "Jam Prods. Is Bringing Back the Bob-Dylan-Willie Nelson Package for Another At-bat This Summer," *Amusement Business,* May 2005, p. 35.

23. Jimmy Leslie, "Def Leppard—Rick Savage Rallies the Rock Brigade," *Bass Player,* June 1, 2005, p. 23.

24. Ibid.

25. Press release, "New Def Leppard Album 'Yeah!' Available for Review," provided by Tracie Galinski, Special Ops Media, May 24, 2006 (May 8, 2007).

26. Ibid.

27. Christa L. Titus, "Def Leppard: Rock On," *Billboard,* June 10, 2006, p. 38.

28. Ray Waddell, "Road Ragers: Five 2007 Tours Likely to Take the Industry by Surprise," *Billboard,* January 6, 2007, p. 29.

29. Press release, "Due to Overwhelming Demand for Tickets From Fans Def Leppard & Journey Announce a Third Leg of Their Current U.S. Tour," provided by Amanda Cagan, ABC Public Relations, August 21, 2006 (May 8, 2007).

30. Ibid.

31. Ray Waddell, "Road Masters: Who's Who Among Finalists for the Billboard Touring Awards," *Billboard,* November 11, 2006, p. 56.

32. Willman.

Chapter 6. "Still on Top of Their Game"

1. Kevin Stein, "Rick Takes the Driver's Seat in His Home Studio," *The Raven Drum*

Foundation, September 2002, <http://www.
ravendrumfoundation.org/interview_rick01.htm>
(January 28, 2008).

2. Carolyn McLuskie, "Music as Medicine: Rick
Allen and Lauren Monroe Share Their Knowledge
at Special Community Drum Circle Saturday,"
Malibu Times, March 22, 2006, p. B1.

3. Ryan O'Quinn, "Def Leppard Drummer Inspires
Many Through Local Foundation," *Malibu Times,*
July 17, 2003, p. B1.

4. Stein.

5. David Fricke, *Def Leppard: Animal Instinct*
(London, England: Zomba Books, 1987), p. 106.

6. "How to change your life," *Men's Fitness,*
February 2007, p. 85.

7. "Biography," *Vivian Campbell,* n.d., <http://www.
viviancampell.com> (January 28, 2008).

8. Philip Anderson, "Joe Elliot—Singer, Def
Leppard," *KAOS,* 2000, <http://www.kaos2000.
net/interviews/defleppard/joeelliott00.html>
(January 28, 2008).

9. Melinda Newman, "What I Did on My London
'Vacation': Radio Report; Def Leppard in the
Studio," *Billboard,* March 11, 1995, p. 12.

10. Press release, "Due to Overwhelming Demand
for Tickets From Fans Def Leppard & Journey
Announce a Third Leg of Their Current U.S.

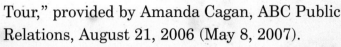

Tour," provided by Amanda Cagan, ABC Public Relations, August 21, 2006 (May 8, 2007).

11. Ibid.

12. "Def Leppard Announces North American Tour," *UPI News Track,* January 11, 2008.

13. Chris Welch, *Def Leppard: Illustrated Biography* (London, England: Omnibus Press, 1984), p. 72.

14. Ibid.

15. Jeremy Helligar, "Talking With . . . Def Leppard's Phil Collen: The Leppard Changes Its Spots," *People Weekly,* May 20, 1996, p. 27.

16. Personal interview with Don Tanner, January 17, 2008.

17. Personal interview with Billy Warden, November 5, 2007.

18. Ibid.

19. Jimmy Leslie, "Def Leppard—Rick Savage Rallies the Rock Brigade," *Bass Player,* June 1, 2005, p. 23.

20. Rob Richard, "Interview: Rick Allen of Def Leppard," *Handidrummed.com,* March 12, 2006, <http://www.handidrummed.com/interviews/ rick_allen.php> (January 31, 2008**).**

21. David Fricke, "Def Leppard Guitarist Found Dead in London Home," *Rolling Stone,* February 21, 1991, p. 14.

22. Chris Willman, "Rock of Ages: Bonus Music Section 2006: Listen to This," *Entertainment Weekly,* May 19, 2006, p. L2T6.

FURTHER READING

Hirschmann, Kris. *The 1980s.* San Diego, Calif.:
Kidhaven Press, 2004.

Kenney, Karen Latchana. *Cool Rock Music: Create and
Appreciate What Makes Music Great!* Edina, Minn.:
ABDO, 2008.

Marcovitz, Hal. *Rock 'n' Roll.* Philadelphia, Penn.: Mason
Crest Publishers, 2003.

Schaefer, A.R. *Forming a Band.* Mankato, Minn.:
Capstone High-Interest Books, 2004.

INTERNET ADDRESSES

Def Leppard: Official Web Site
<http://www.defleppard.com/>

Def Leppard
<http://www.rollingstone.com/artists/defleppard>

INDEX